"HERMAN IS NOT CHIC.
HE IS NOT COOL.

He is not one of the Beautiful People. . . . Herman is the universal schlemeil—a bit of you, a touch of your boss, a smattering of your brother-in-law and a lot of Jim Unger."
—*Washington Star*

"One of North America's hottest comic artists. . . . The low, mean wit of Jim Unger makes HERMAN uncommonly hilarious."
—*Chicago Tribune*

"The belly bulges, the nose is protuberant and the back is invariably hunched. The image is unmistakable. In black and white or color, in English or in German, Herman is a cartoon character who provides a daily dosage of levity and subtlety for addicted readers around the world."
—*Ottawa Citizen*

"Herman is lower middle class, but at the same time he can be a doctor or bank president. . . . He is everybody. . . . Herman is universal. But above all, Herman is outrageous. And there lies his fame."
—*Orlando Sentinel Star*

More Big Laughs from SIGNET

"And you wonder, Herman, why I never want to go to Italian restaurants!"

by

Jim Unger

A SIGNET BOOK

NEW AMERICAN LIBRARY

TIMES MIRROR

Published by arrangement with Andrews and McMeel, Inc. The Andrews and
McMeel edition of "And You Wonder, Herman, Why I Never Want to
Go to Italian Restaurants!" was published simultaneously in Canada by
Gage Publishing

"Herman" is syndicated internationally by UNIVERSAL PRESS SYNDICATE

"You're not Robert Redford."

"We'll take you off the vitamins for
a couple of days."

"Well, now we know what all that noise was about last night."

"This one's not signed."

"Members of the jury, have you reached a verdict?"

"I'll come back later when you're not busy."

"Will you quit arguing and give me my seven iron."

"Couldn't resist, could you?"

"Your mother warned me you'd start complaining about your food."

"I thought you said you were coming home
next Sunday"

"Is there anything you need before I go?"

"It's the cook's coffee-break, so eat your
dessert first."

"Try to guess who this is for..."

"ONE."

"Is that your idea of 20 pounds of potatoes?"

"34-24-36...It sounds like your right arm."

"Sure, I'd love a second honeymoon...who with?"

"Want me to wrap it?"

"Sorry to keep you both waiting out here. Where's your wife?"

"Whaddya making?"

"Want mashed potatoes?"

"If I've gotta do typing and stuff like that, I want
more money!"

"Get up, you idiot. When I say, 'how do you plead?'
I wanna know if you're 'guilty' or 'not guilty'."

"How much longer did he tell you to stay on this banana diet?"

"That new guy was supposed to be helping me roll this."

"Haven't you got a brush?"

"I know you're in bed with the flu, but I need the
keys to the filing cabinet."

"Your four aces don't beat my two eights unless
you've got a red king!"

"Think it'll work?"

"Try to relax."

"You're supposed to say 'I do' not 'I'll try.'"

"Did you sleep okay, Herman?"

"Your mother said you loved eggs for breakfast!"

"Listen, I gotta go. There's a guy waiting to use the phone."

"All I said was I didn't want it in stereo."

"Two of these just fell out of the car."

"Did he make you buy anything?"

"'One Hundred and One Ways to Rip Off Credit Companies'... is that cash or charge?"

"I make it a rule never to lend money to people who borrow!"

"What song did you sing?"

"Had any luck?"

"Don't forget to lock up when you leave, Henderson."

"I'd expect it from the younger generation, but asking for more money at your age is absolutely inexcusable."

"Can I take them with water?"

"I was in the neighborhood and I thought I'd drop
in for a couple of weeks."

"It comes with a guarantee for five years or until
you use it, whichever comes first."

"I'll work my way up your arm and you tell
me when you feel anything."

"Is that the only way you can have a good time,
smashing up public property?"

"Show me that piece of paper again with the calculations on it."

"The man we're looking for will be dynamic
and aggressive."

"Three nights in a row I've dreamt
you were Dracula."

"Is that the tie I bought him for Christmas?"

"Do I get that one again?"

"He loves a cup of tea."

"Shall I turn it off?"

"I read somewhere that expensive champagne
doesn't go 'pop.'"

"I don't care if it is plastic. I could have had
a heart attack."

"Night work! You mean when it's dark?"

"Have you got any others with more spikes?"

"The sporting goods store phoned. You left your hat on the counter."

"Madam, giving your husband 'twenty years in the slammer' is not my idea of a divorce settlement."

"STAMPEDE!"

"Why don't you start climbing out and I'll keep
trying the buttons."

"I'm your anesthetist and he's my 'back-up man'."

"Stay calm...I'm gonna get a second opinion on
your blood pressure."

"Sure it's big, but it'll do an average room in three minutes."

"Your wife took the new baby home in a cab
an hour ago."

"You're certainly enjoying my little cakes. Have
another one!"

"Hold it! They're out of season."

"I take it you don't want any of this cheese."

"I'll only be gone for a month, so don't use the kitchen."

"There goes my tip, right?"

"Members of the jury, I ask you—does my client look like a man of violence?"

"Wanna see the list of optional extras?"

"Your plane's been delayed ten minutes. A couple of rivets popped loose."

"Here, you wanted a shark's-tooth necklace.
Dig those outa my leg."

"Next time your car won't start, try calling a mechanic."

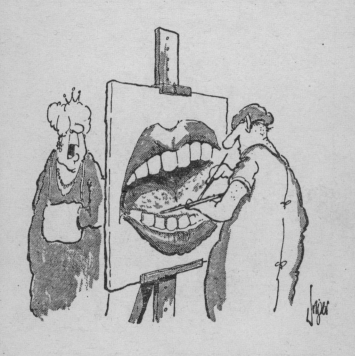

"For the money I'm paying for this portrait, I hope you're getting beneath the surface and painting the real me."

"How come I never hear you say 'please' and
'thank-you'."

"This is my new boyfriend. Can he have something to eat?"

"He'll be okay! He overdosed on sunflower seeds."

"Good grief man! How does anyone swallow an
electric toothbrush?"

"Yeah, well your not exactly an oil painting yourself
first thing in the morning."

"Are you sure he told you to stick a barometer in my mouth?"

"If you don't believe men came from monkeys, go and take a good look at your father."

"Did you make a blind date with someone
named Yvonne?"

"Herman, here's your ax back. Now can I borrow your chain saw?"

"Of course it's dangerous. I didn't get to be a general without taking chances."

"Come on, don't waste my time. Get out of there."

"Mind your own business! This is how I like it."

ABOUT THE AUTHOR

JIM UNGER was born in London, England. After surviving the blitz bombings of World War II and two years in the British Army, followed by a short career as a London bobby and a driving instructor, he immigrated to Canada in 1968, where he became a newspaper graphic artist and editorial cartoonist. For three years running he won the Ontario Weekly Newspaper Association's "Cartoonist of the Year" award. In 1974 he began drawing HERMAN for Universal Press Syndicate, with instant popularity. HERMAN is now enjoyed by 60 million daily and Sunday newspaper readers all around the world. The cartoon collections THE HERMAN TREASURIES became paperback bestsellers.

Jim Unger now lives in Nassau, Bahamas.